TO

_____

FROM

_____

DATE

_____

JOURNAL

be still
+ know

PSALM 46:10

a future + a hope

JEREMIAH 29:11

created by
the word of God

HEBREWS 11:1-3

*wait for the salvation
of the LORD*

LAMENTATIONS 3:26

rejoice in hope

ROMANS 5:2

His mercies never stop

LAMENTATIONS 3:22-23

draw near

HEBREWS 10:22

My kindness is all you need

II CORINTHIANS 12:9

let your
light shine

MATTHEW 5:16

Walk by faith

II CORINTHIANS 5:7

He will shelter you

PSALM 91:4

His divine power

II PETER 1:3

more than conquerors

ROMANS 8:35, 37-39

fill my cup

PSALM 23:5-6

newness of life

ROMANS 6:4

love never fails!

I CORINTHIANS 13:8

God can do much, much more

EPHESIANS 3:20

hope is in the Lord

PSALM 146:5

His face shine upon you

NUMBERS 6:25

nothing will be impossible

MATTHEW 17:20

His purposes never change

HEBREWS 6:17, 18

give you the power

II THESSALONIANS 1:11

chosen you

COLOSSIANS 3:12

encourage one another

I THESSALONIANS 5:11

greatest of these is love

I CORINTHIANS 13:13

abundant joy

PSALM 16:11

rejoice and be glad

PSALM 90:14

renew your life

RUTH 4:15

He laid down His life

I JOHN 3:16

Greater love

JOHN 15:13

take heart

JOHN 16:33

overflow with hope

ROMANS 15:13

God's love has been poured out

ROMANS 5:5

blessed hope

TITUS 2:13

that you may know

EPHESIANS 1:18-19

god loves you

I THESSALONIANS 1:4

saved through faith

EPHESIANS 2:8

be an example

I TIMOTHY 4:12

do what is good PSALM 37:3

give thanks to the LORD

I CHRONICLES 16:34

His faithful love

may have life

JOHN 10:10

god... blesses us

I TIMOTHY 6:17

shine as lights

PHILIPPIANS 2:15-16

blessing of life

PSALM 133:3

Celebrate with great joy

NEHEMIAH 8:12

many blessings

PROVERBS 28:20

comfort your hearts

II THESSALONIANS 2:16-17

I am with you always

MATTHEW 28:20

anchor of the soul

HEBREWS 6:19

Glory be to God!

He is faithful

HEBREWS 10:23

more like Him

II CORINTHIANS 3:18

love
one
another

I JOHN 4:7

fulfilled in Christ

II CORINTHIANS 1:20

example of their faith

HEBREWS 13:7

prospering in every way

III JOHN 1:2

His love for us

always with you

ZEPHANIAH 3:17

Kingdom of god

ROMANS 14:17

grace +
peace

II PETER 1:2

share in the comfort

Your love never fails

PSALM 138:8

strengthen your heart

The LORD is good

LAMENTATIONS 3:25

hope in god!

PSALM 42:11

our eyes on Jesus

HEBREWS 12:1, 2

He is God

DEUTERONOMY 7:9

give
thanks
in
everything

I THESSALONIANS 5:18

His faithful ones

I have loved you

JEREMIAH 31:3

Light of the world

JOHN 8:12

He makes me glad

ACTS 2:28

In Him was life

JOHN 1:4

Rejoice in every day

ECCLESIASTES 11:8

walk in love

EPHESIANS 5:2

a hope that lives on

I PETER 1:3

the glory of His inheritance

EPHESIANS 1:18

written in Your book

PSALM 139:16

This is the victory

I JOHN 5:4

love never gives up

I CORINTHIANS 13:7

every good thing

PHILEMON 1:6

great is Your faithfulness

LAMENTATIONS 3:22-23

*great
joy*

LUKE 2:10

The Lord leads

PSALM 25:10

god is love

I JOHN 4:16

god is my helper

PSALM 54:4

My Life is in Your hands

goodness and mercy

PSALM 23:6

I will care for you

ISAIAH 46:4

light and joy

PROVERBS 13:9

I will guide you

PSALM 32:8

restores
my soul

PSALM 23:3

fills my life

PSALM 103:5

For I Know the Plans Journal
© 2019 DaySpring Cards, Inc. All rights reserved.
First Edition, May 2019

Published by:

P.O. Box 1010
Siloam Springs, AR 72761
dayspring.com

Lettering by Shelby Taylor
Illustration by Alisa Hipp
Design by Lauren Purtle

Printed in China

Prime: 94312

ISBN: 978-1-64454-295-8